Folding Instructions and Diagrams
STAGE 1

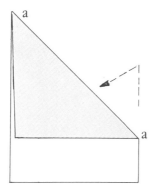

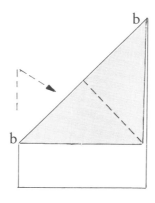

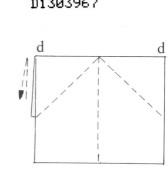

1. Lay cut-out flier flat. Fold top corner down to opposite side (*aa*).

2. Open flat and repeat on opposite corner (*bb*).

3. Open flat and fold vertically through the center (*cc*).

4. Open flat and fold on horizontal (*dd*).

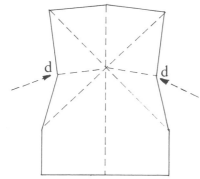

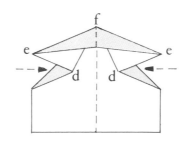

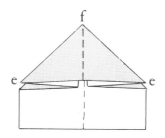

5. Open flat and begin lifting at sides of horizontal fold (*dd*).

6. Continue lifting to form triangle *efe*.

7. Press *efe* flat, making sure it is symmetrical.

STAGE 2

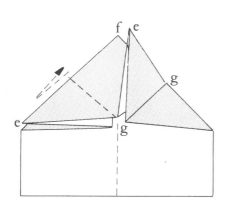

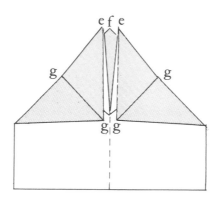

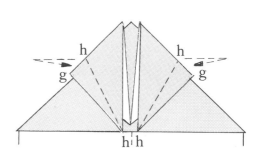

8. Working on triangle *efe*, raise one side of triangle (point *e*) to top (*f*), pressing fold on *gg*.

9. Repeat on other side, pressing both points *e* flat at *f*.

10. Fold both points *g* to middle on lines *hh*.

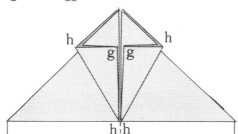

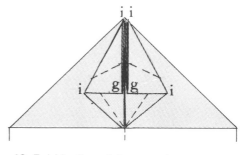

11. Press flat, then open out.

12. Fold both points *gg* again to center, this time from top on lines *ii*.

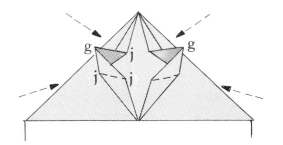

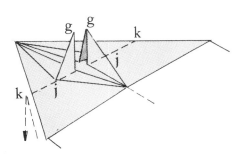

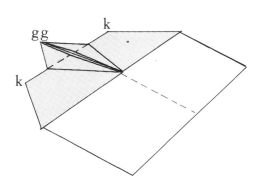

13. Open flat. Pinch and raise points *gg*, making extra-sharp folds on both sides at lines *jj*. Use ruler edge if necessary to sharpen these folds.

14. With triangles *gjj* folded firmly upright, fold nose down at line *kk*. Press flat.

15. Points *gg* will come together to form nose of stunt flier.

STAGE 3

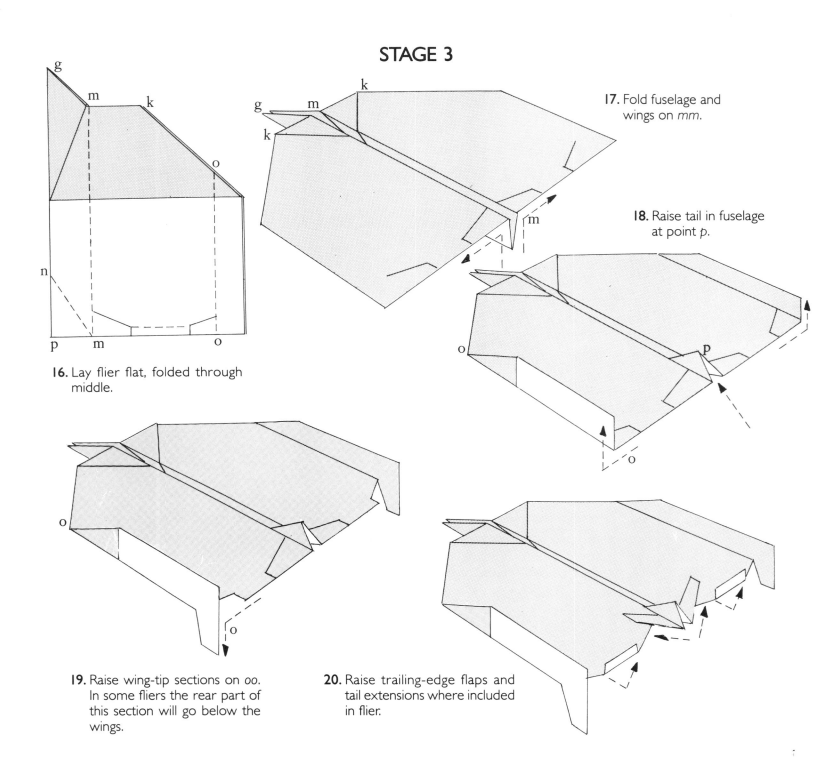

17. Fold fuselage and wings on *mm*.

18. Raise tail in fuselage at point *p*.

16. Lay flier flat, folded through middle.

19. Raise wing-tip sections on *oo*. In some fliers the rear part of this section will go below the wings.

20. Raise trailing-edge flaps and tail extensions where included in flier.

DIAGRAMS OF INDIVIDUAL FLIERS FOLLOW PLATES

2. Advanced Space Trainer

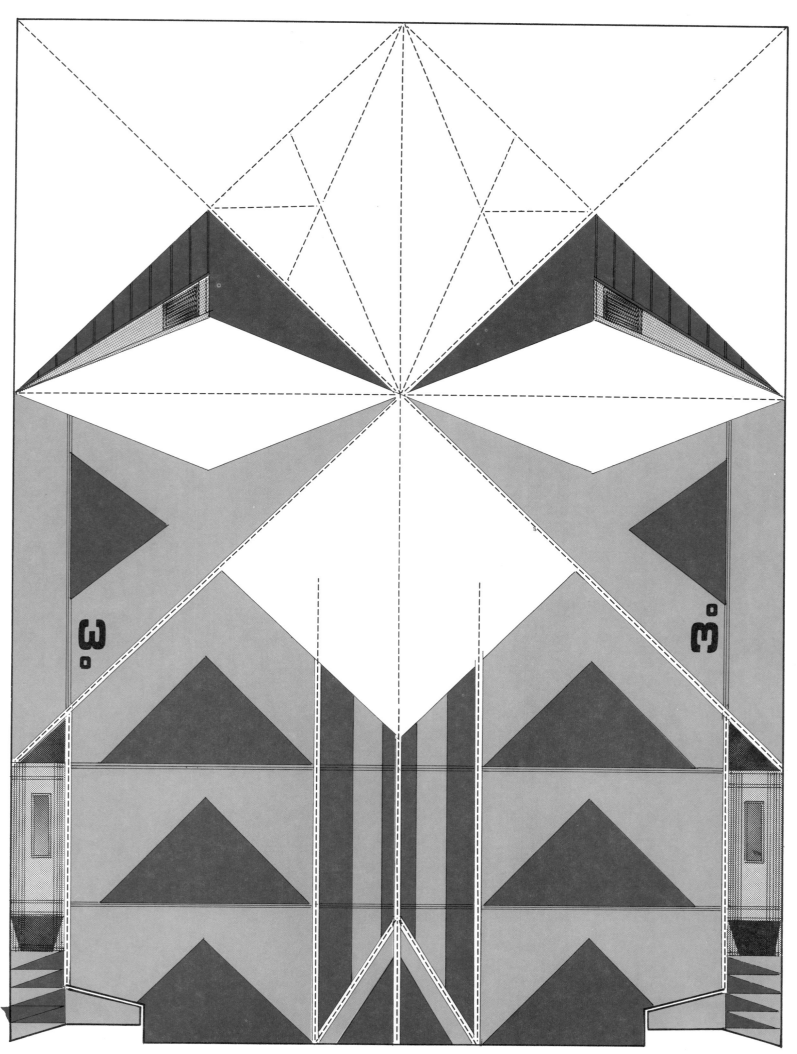

3. Space Venturer

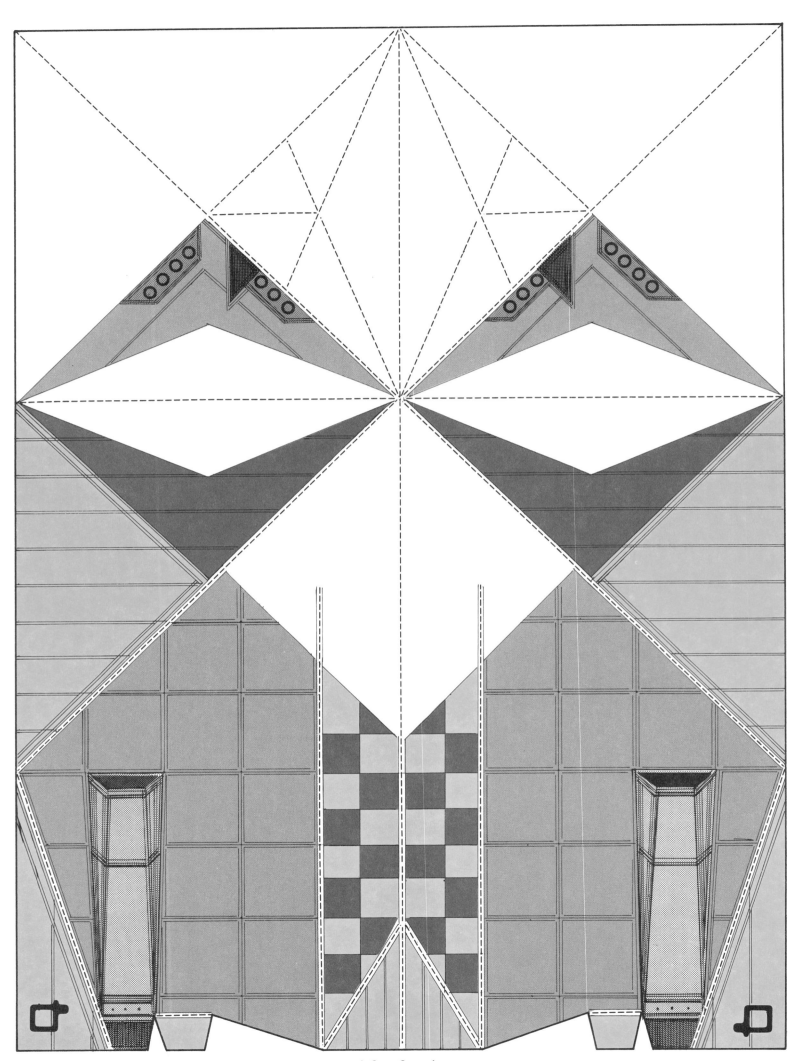

4. Star Searcher

5. Intruder Patrol

6. Space Scout

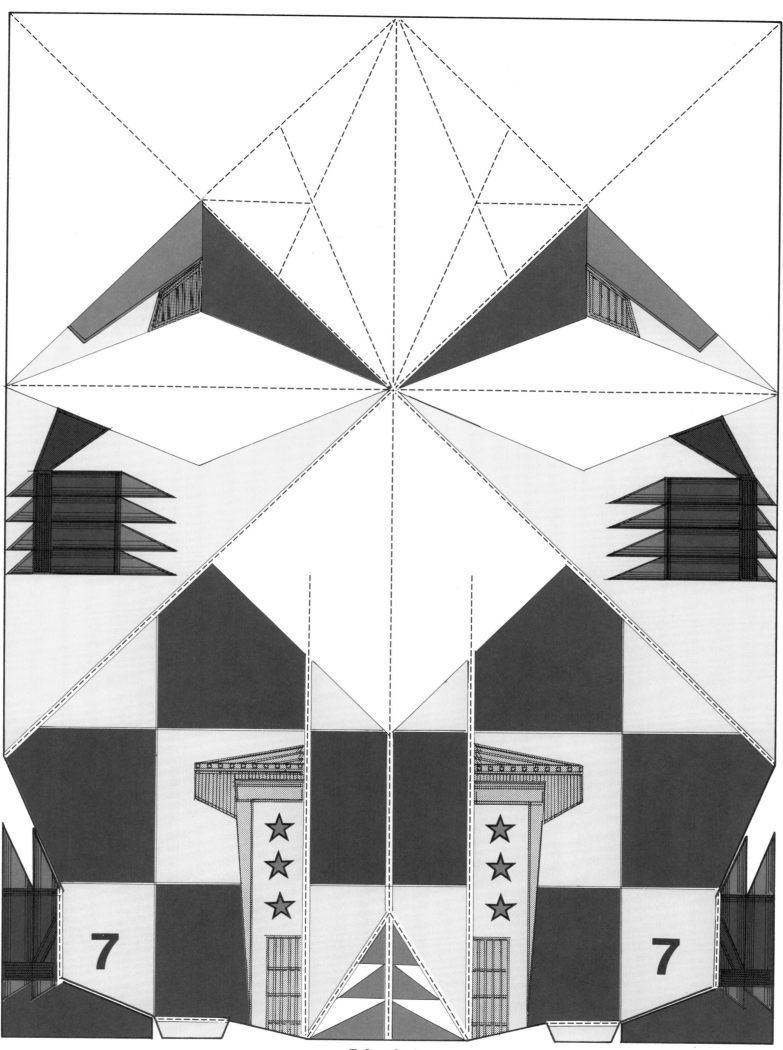

7. Star Strike

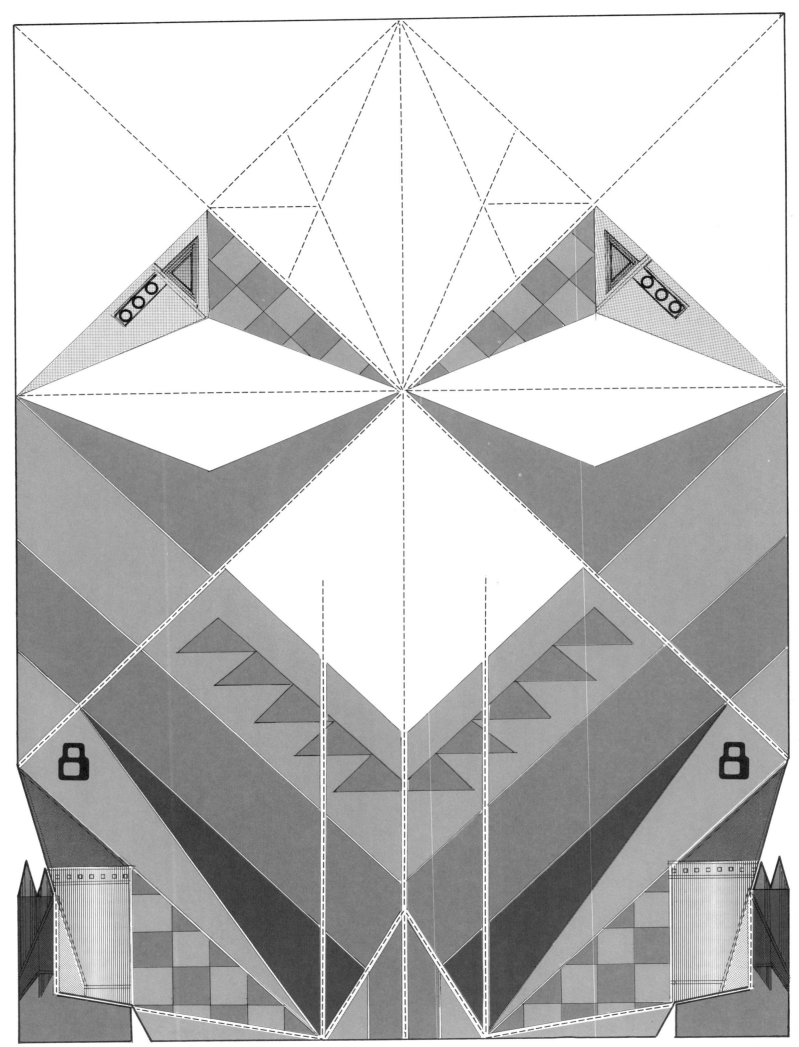

8. Star Link

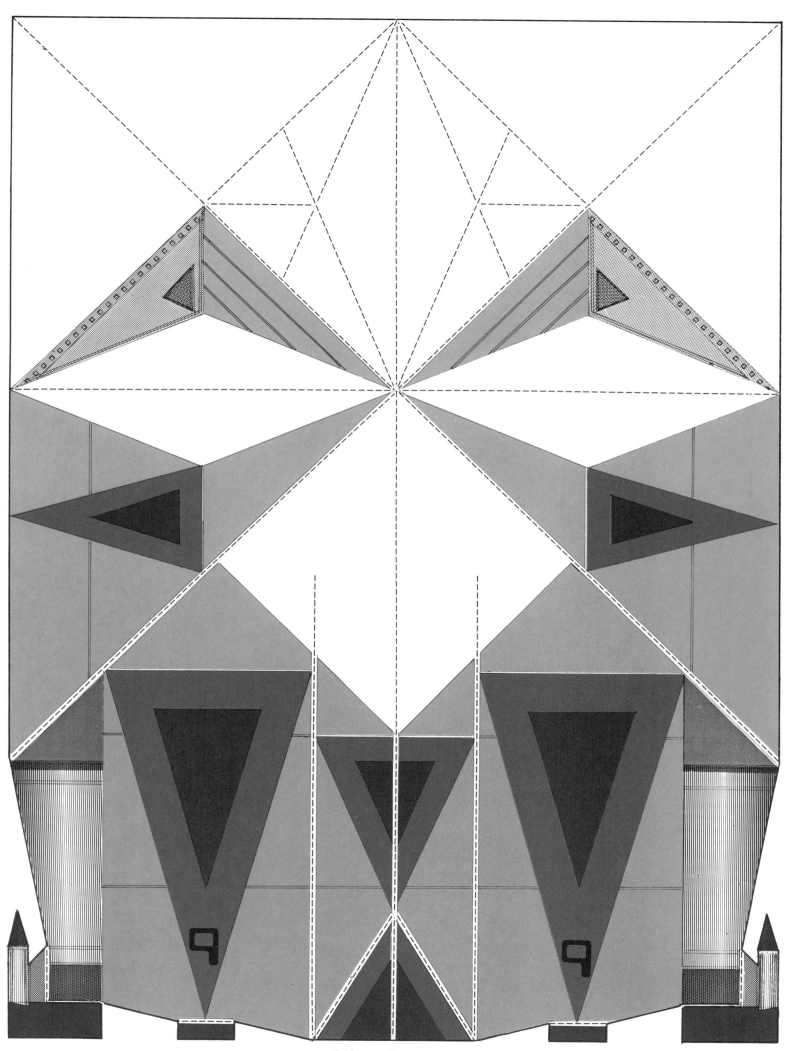

9. Space Penetrator

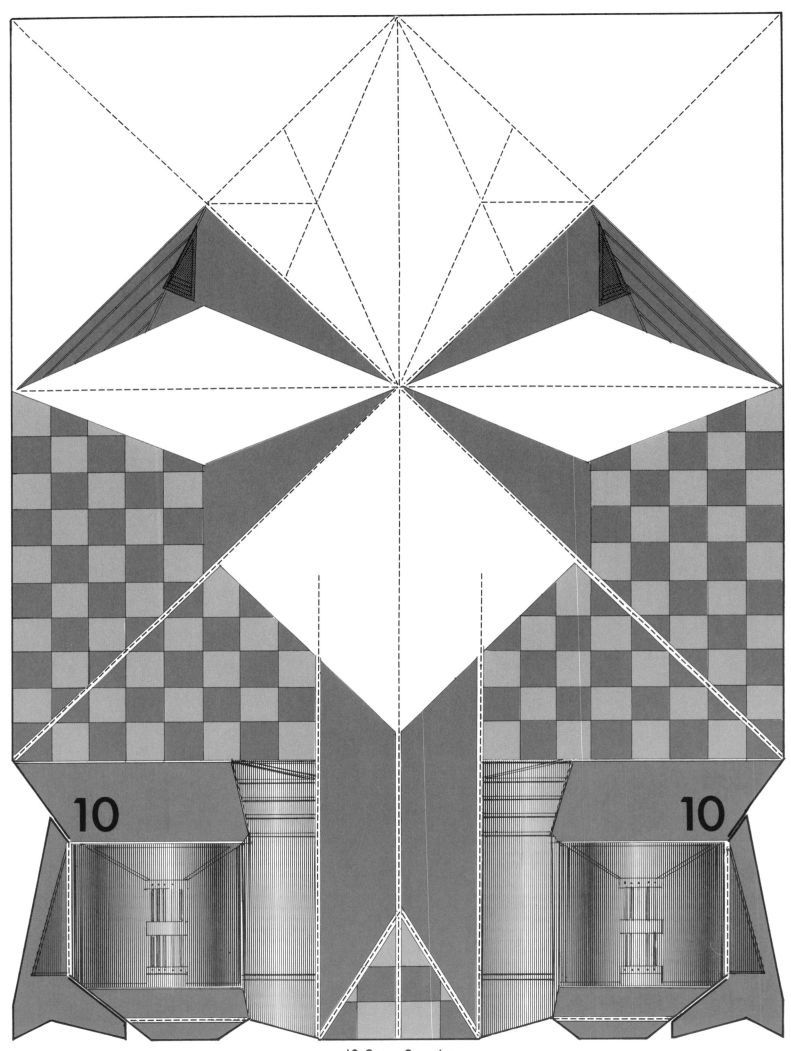

10. Space Sounder

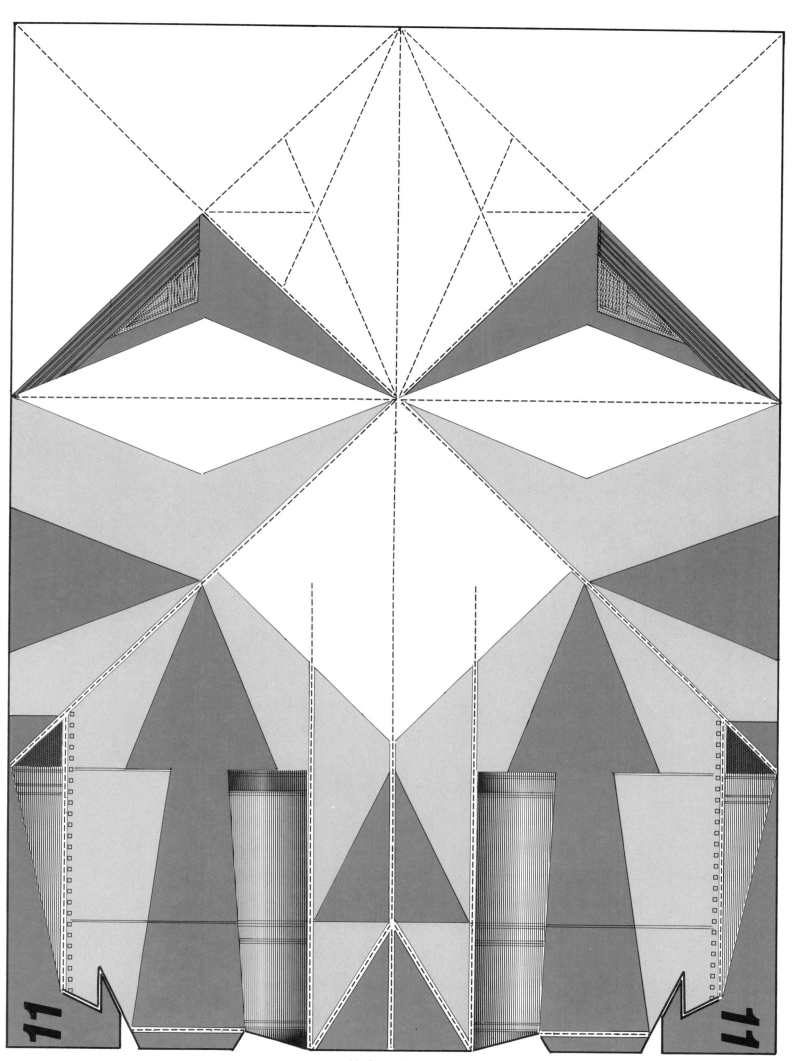

11. Star Circler

12. Star Thunderer

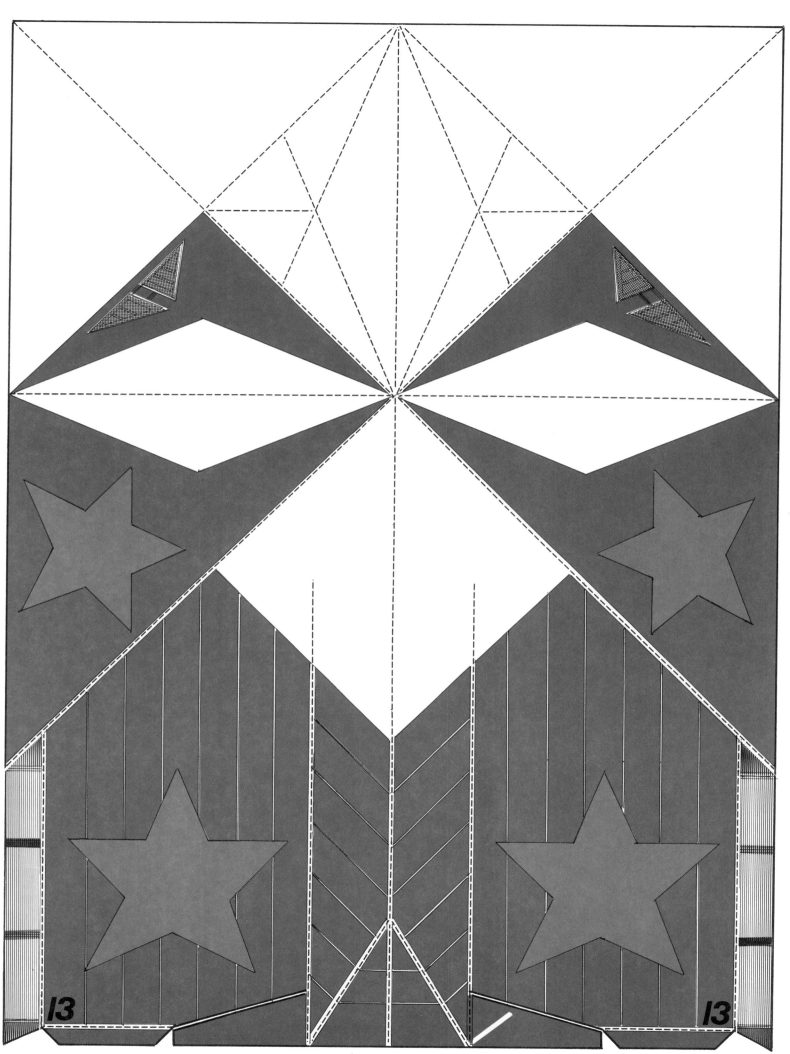

13. Deep Space Probe

14. Space Connector

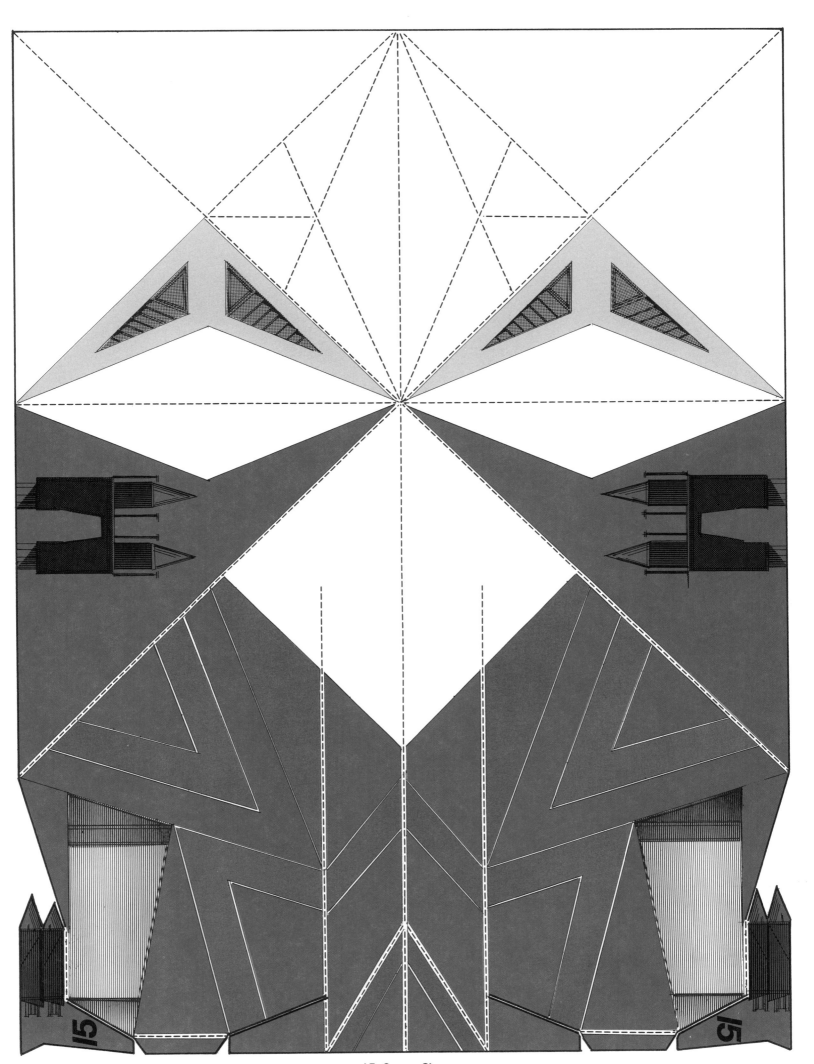

15. Space Slam

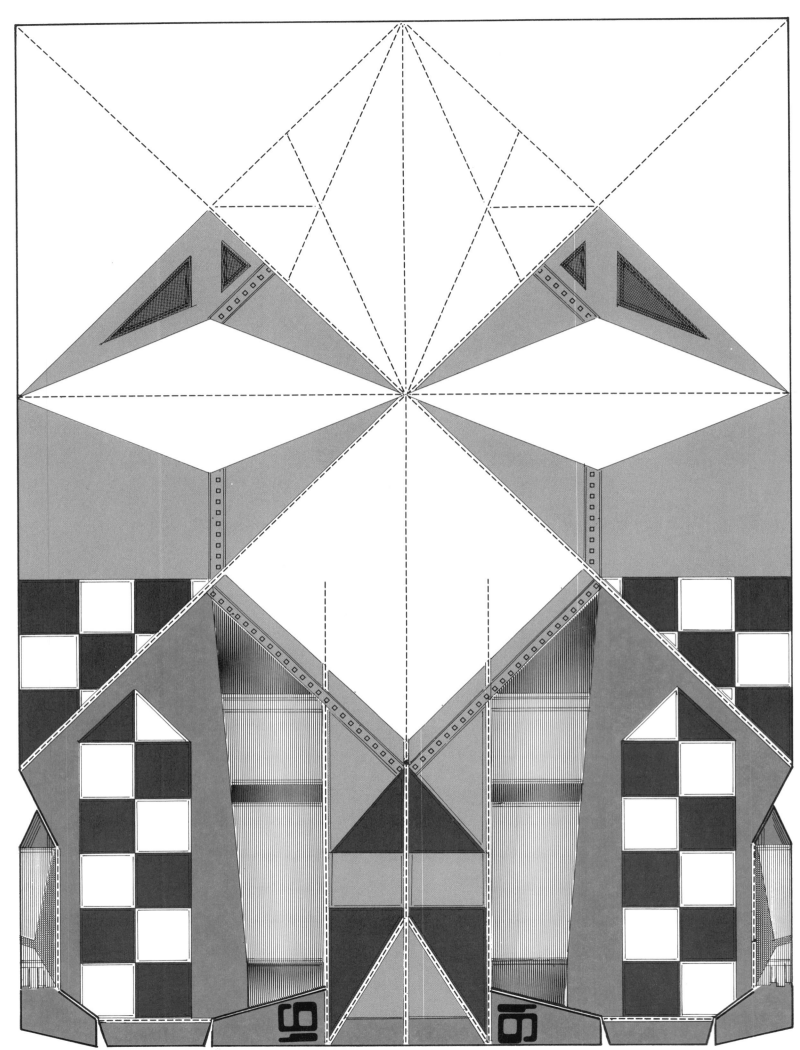

16. Satellite Control

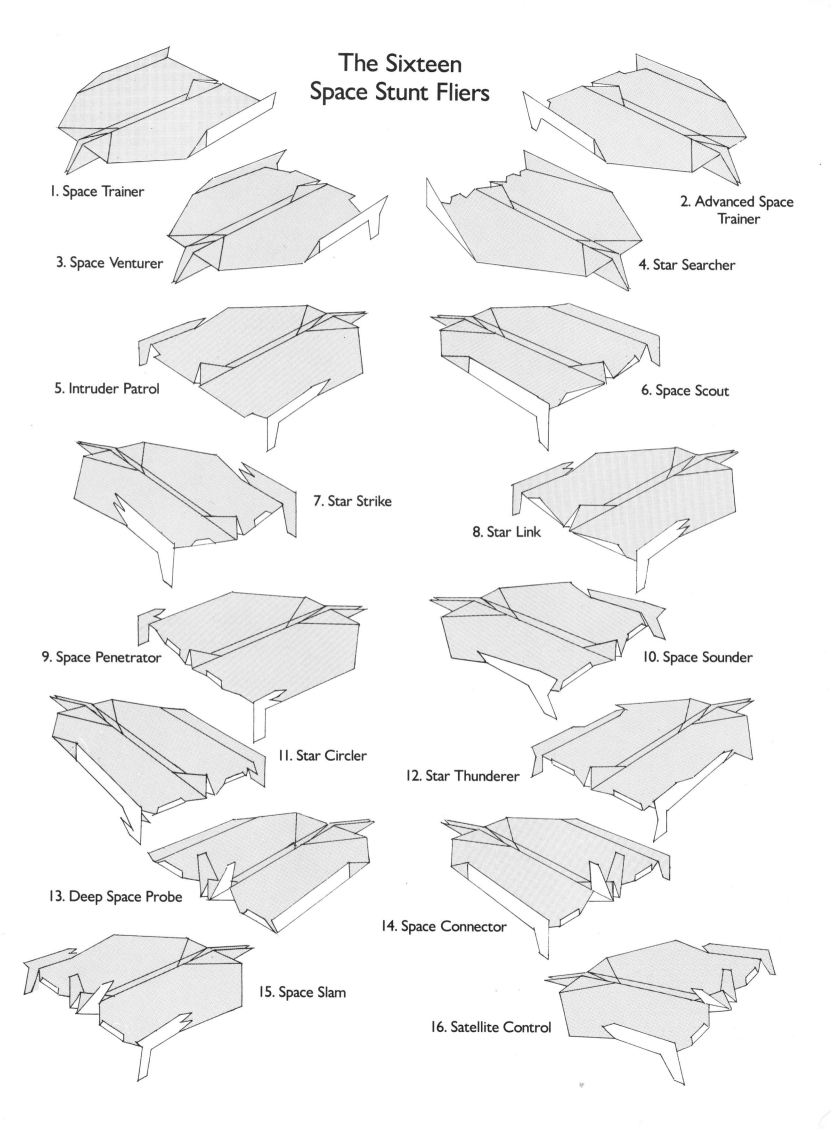

The Sixteen
Space Stunt Fliers

1. Space Trainer

2. Advanced Space
   Trainer

3. Space Venturer

4. Star Searcher

5. Intruder Patrol

6. Space Scout

7. Star Strike

8. Star Link

9. Space Penetrator

10. Space Sounder

11. Star Circler

12. Star Thunderer

13. Deep Space Probe

14. Space Connector

15. Space Slam

16. Satellite Control